ISLAND
WHIMSY

ISLAND WHIMSY

CELERIE KEMBLE

DESIGNING A PARADISE BY THE SEA

RIZZOLI NEW YORK

New York · Paris · London · Milan

To Delio,

who had all the best moves,
made the most of every minute,
and shared his heart, smile,
and dreams so generously.

CONTENTS

A Long Walk Down the Beach

A house by the sea should be a house of dreams. Where windows and doors are thrown open to the ocean, and gusts of cool, salty air turn us all into kids again—buoyant and joyful. Free. To paraphrase Isak Dinesen, when I'm at the beach, I think: *Here I am. Where I belong.*

Growing up in Florida, I spent much of my childhood in a damp, sandy bathing suit, my hair crispy with salt, my back streaked with bands of sunburn from hastily applied Coppertone. I'm intimately familiar with the joy of carrying a to-go cup of white wine out to the ocean at sunset, tying the hem of my dress into a knot as my heels sink into the sand at the surf line. Over the years, I've been lucky enough to have my work as a designer take me to coasts from Nantucket to Naples, Malibu to the Caribbean.

Each of these places has its own delights, from the funky Dungeness crab shack at the Ventura County line in California to the magical pine forests of Northeast Harbor, Maine. But I've never responded to any beach the way I did to Playa Grande. It was like nothing I'd ever seen before: a wild swath of mountainous jungle on the Dominican Republic's northern coast, rolling down to pastures of clear, wobbling minty-blue water, banded together by a downy crescent of golden sand that seemed to go on forever. As soon as I saw it, I thought: *Oh no. I am in trouble.*

It was the summer of 2004, and my fiancé and I had flown down to the DR at the behest of my beloved Dominican friend Delio Gonzales. Delio knew Playa Grande (which was for sale) and insisted we see it. He had long been familiar with our dream of building a group of vacation homes with friends and family. The fantasy was that it would be somewhere beautiful and wild but not too remote. A place where we could build a cluster of houses centered around a shared clubhouse, which would perhaps turn into a boutique hotel when the homes weren't in use. Whenever we traveled somewhere we loved, we'd visit various properties that were for sale and engage in endless discussions about the merits of each option. But, to be honest, I thought of it mostly as a recreational fantasy—I didn't expect anything to materialize. ⎯

Then we stepped out onto the sand of Playa Grande, and I felt my spine glow with excitement.

It's not right to say that Playa Grande was a "virgin" beach, or that it was "untouched." The place is cherished by locals and has a history going back centuries to the Taino Indians who lived on the beach's sheltered sands. As we walked, kids jumped around in the shallows and surfers unzipped the turquoise waves down at the far end of the beach; families picnicked under umbrellas. Fishermen walked along the beach with trays, selling red snapper and octopus and oysters fresh out of the ocean, their dazzling colors displayed on ice.

I couldn't help imagining my own children (children I didn't yet have, mind you) frolicking in the waves, too, my family and friends gathered around a bonfire, counting constellations and mosquito bites—walking up the beach at the end of the night to a home we could return to year after year.

But the idea scared me, too. I'd never built in the Caribbean before, spoke only fifth-grade Spanish (and remembered that report card column filled with C's), and struggled with the enormity and responsibility of changing this deeply precious place. I thought: *Is there a way to thread this needle correctly? To build something that is both humble and inspiring? A place that doesn't take away from the sense of expansiveness and wonder and gratitude that this beach evokes but bows down before it? Something that, instead of imposing upon what already exists, feels almost evolved from it?*

I grew up in a pretty magical place—one that has been carefully built and curated by four generations of my family. My great-great-grandparents were some of the first settlers on the island of Palm Beach back in the late 1800s, when it was still swamp and sawgrass. I spent my childhood on a rambling property with a bunch of old family houses, surrounded by acres of jungle overlooking the part of the Intracoastal known as Lake Worth. We lived in a deconsecrated church—a beautiful but gangly wood-shingled Gothic building with an octagonal clock tower and multiple shingled porches decked out in floral chintz and wicker, open to the lake on one side and the jungle on the other. My great-grandparents' house next door was a white Victorian kit house, frilly with doily-like woodwork. As a teenager, I fantasized that our property was the love child of Isabel Allende and John Irving, combining generations of Latin passion and New England eccentricity with a shared love of home. Nothing was palatial or pristine or gilded the way the great houses of Palm Beach are, but it was—and is—a monument to romantic chaos that I have come to think of as the embodiment of home.

We were a family defined by sand on the kitchen floor and in the creases of our car seats. There was always bougainvillea crawling in the windows. Always a cheese weeping on the kitchen counter. People dropped by in wet bathing suits, fresh from the beach, and stayed for sunset cocktails. At night, I fell asleep to the sound of bamboo creaking outside my windows, frogs singing in the trees.

But our house was a place of elegance and comfort too. The silver was never polished, but there was a many-generations-deep collection of it. The floors had been

hand-painted by my mother and father. The pink-and-green tiles imported from Portugal. The sheets pressed and fragrant. How this lovely balance was achieved won't come as a surprise to anyone. My mother, Mimi McMakin, is a legend in the world of interiors. Gracious and warm, witty and wildly creative, she may be the best-known decorator in Palm Beach. And her gift for conjuring spaces that are simultaneously whimsical and welcoming has inspired me for as long as I can remember.

When I began to imagine building homes at Playa Grande, I envisioned a similar kind of enchantment: a wild, romantic place that was also modest in scale and appropriate to the location. I hoped my family and I might gently weave ourselves into the vibrant community that was already there, summoning the spirit of my childhood home through the lens of the Caribbean landscape and the Dominican culture.

I knew it would be a big undertaking. I was used to decorating houses and apartments. Now we were talking about building a resort. From the ground up. I remember the early plans and exuberance, at times imagining we could have the houses built in a few years, only to realize: *No way. This will take a decade.* But I was caught, because I loved imagining it. I'd never designed a project without a client—something based purely on my own taste and desire and my interpretations of the people closest to me—and the idea thrilled me. I wanted to create a retreat where we could easily surf and swim and dance and dream and recuperate. Pretty, but casual. A little group of houses gathered around a lawn. A pool overlooking the ocean. A garden full of tropical flowers with the big wooly shoulders of the jungle rising up beyond. I loved how the jungle came frothing right down to the sand, with the sea grapes and almond leaves flashing in the sun and the steep blond cliffs at the far end, the coconut palms arcing out over the sand. Every time I saw the beach, it made me want to throw my head back and sing.

As my fiancé and I talked more about what the resort might look like, we thought: *What about something low and open? Two stories only. No walls. No fences. Inclusive. Meandering, with the beach easily open to the public.*

I think good design is always a marriage of self and setting. A home exists first and foremost to make its inhabitants feel safe and comfortable—to tell stories about the things they love and the times they've shared, and to help inspire them to do new things. But the best houses also tell a story about the place itself, the landscape and the larger culture within which its inhabitants live.

When it came time to design our property at Playa Grande, I thought not only of my great-grandparents' triple-gabled house in Florida, but also of the colorful Victorians west of us in Puerto Plata, and the farmhouses

up in the hills with their rustic hand-carved woodwork. These were decorative elements authentic to the Dominican Republic and fantastically suited to the breezes, sun-blasts, storms, and jungle settings. Another source of inspiration were English set designer Oliver Messel's wonderful follies on Mustique and Turks and Caicos, which invite the landscape in with their open French doors and pastel plantation shutters and their porches constructed around the lazy elbows of long-armed trees.

I thought of the lush magical realism of Gabriel García Márquez novels, where nature is as much a character as any of the humans, and where memory and fantasy are as present in the air as humidity or thunder. It was that sense of spirit and play that I wanted to impart to whoever came to Playa Grande—the feeling you get when you've been barefoot somewhere for three days with very bad cell reception and very good cocktails. The kind that gets under your skin.

As it turns out, it would be another seven years before construction even began at Playa Grande. But because we had the luxury of time, I was able to slowly accumulate wonderfully odd objects from flea markets and antiques shops and art fairs during my travels. These were things that felt special to me but weren't necessarily expensive, many of them one-of-a-kind pieces like an antique wicker canopy daybed (I can never have enough daybeds) or the pair of stone lions beside the pool that now roar down the beach in opposite directions. To this pile I added a needlepoint ottoman made by my grandmother, and some deliciously rusted metal flowers from Spain whose combination of beauty and decay made my fingers tingle, along with a stack of vintage Porthault linens that zoomed me right back to the floral bedrooms of my 1970s childhood.

Pieces that spark memories or hopes for the future come together over time to form the soul of a home, and they're the one element a decorator can't easily provide for you. The good news, though, is that these items are, by their very nature, things that will thrill you and make your heart beat a little faster, so the journey of gathering them should be a long and pleasurable one. This is especially true when you're collecting treasures for a coastal house, where sea glass and sand dollars, peach-speckled crab shells and driftwood found on beach walks signify not just beauty but lazy, screen-free afternoons spent by the ocean with loved ones. Increasingly precious commodities in this day and age!

During the years that Playa Grande was being built, my fiancé and I married and added our three children—Rascal, Zinnia, and Wick—to our family. And we quickly developed a tradition of bringing them, along with a bunch of our friends, down to the DR every New Year's, setting up camp on the beach and shuttling into town to join the dancing and midnight fireworks. Slowly, the big pieces of the Playa Grande "club" began to fall into place.

The chapters of this book are organized around the different ways I sought to braid my family's story into the larger landscape of Playa Grande and to provide inspiration, joy, and respite to all who come. "Fantasy" looks at the way we used whimsical, dreamlike elements—from the latticework cabanas by the pool to the lamb statues on the property who "mow" the lawns—throughout the property to create a sense of play and possibility. "Light, Salt, Air" describes how we went about bringing the most precious elements of the beach into the homes themselves, creating a feeling of flow and permeability, and reminding you constantly of where you are.

"In the Jungle" looks at the design cues I took from the flora and fauna of the tropical rainforest surrounding Playa Grande to create an alluring tension between chaos and refinement. "Sweet & Dark" examines the surprising color combinations that tango into life in the tropics—whether in the form of tribal prints in hot Gauguin colors mixed with Jordan-almond pastels or handmade objects like a papier-mâché lobster mask that brings a shout of spirit to a room. Finally, "Texture" focuses on the powerful impact that thoughtfully layered materials—from rough, local coquina stone and painted antique wicker to the smooth polished cotton of Dutch wax prints—have on a space.

Viewed together, these five chapters add up to a rough recipe for my idea of island style. But really, the key ingredient is love. I am aware that "love" is an abstract and potentially fey-sounding term for a designer to toss about as a principle of design. I stand by it, though, and in an attempt to express my feelings about Playa Grande more directly, I have included quotations and excerpts from some of my favorite poems—ones that gave energy and inspiration to the design work and hopefully convey some of the sincere love and wonder I feel towards the property.

If you have a house at the beach (or hope to have one someday), you'll want to look to the natural landscape around you for cues about which colors and materials will bloom most happily there—and then pick the ones that speak to you. Similarly, you'll want to consider and find ways to incorporate the spirit of the place itself, the unique culture and traditions within which you've chosen to live or vacation, whether in the form of watercolors by a local artist or fisherman's buoys and sun-faded flags you found at a nearby vintage shop. But by far the most important thing—the ingredient that will thread all these elements into a beautiful, unique space—is you. Your specific joys and tastes and preferences and hobbies and memories and dreams (and those of your family members) are the glue that will hold everything together. They are the secret difference between a house and a home.

I'll never forget looking down the beach that first day at Playa Grande and realizing that we were going to go for it: take a risk and fall in love; give it everything we had. I remember the intoxication of possibility, the heart-knocking fear and excitement, the sense that having had a vision, we would now cleave to it. I peered into the jungle and saw a triple-gabled roof rising up from the trees. I saw my friends and family gathered around the pool. I heard my children, far out in the future, laughing. I walked toward them.

FOLLOWING PAGES
Paloma, the alpha beach dog of Playa Grande, surveys her domain. She was there when we first started coming to the Dominican Republic fifteen years ago, and she immediately began accompanying us on our late-afternoon walks down the beach. Soon the other beach dogs would fall in behind her, and by the end of the walk, there'd be half a dozen of them with us, enjoying the sunset.

Fantasy

In the beginning of *Willy Wonka and the Chocolate Factory,* Gene Wilder's character tells his young guests, "We are the music makers, and we are the dreamers of dreams." That's the way Playa Grande made me feel the first time I saw it, and I wanted to share this feeling of possibility and magic with everyone who came. The project started out as a fantasy. I found myself envisioning buildings that were dreamlike in their whimsy and romance: as light and pretty as lace-like paper doilies rising up from the jungle, yet sturdy and functional at the same time.

I grew up in a kind of folly. Our family home in Palm Beach is an old wooden church with morning glories curling in the windows and thirty-foot cathedral ceilings. I know how inspiring it is to spend time in a space like that, how beauty and fantasy encourage the mind to soar and dream, and I will never tire of trying to bring those things into people's lives. When it came time to imagine a folly for our time, I was greatly inspired by the Victorian houses in Puerto Plata, a nearby town in the Dominican Republic. With their ornate woodwork, they felt both pretty and appealingly rustic. I also looked to combine what was beautiful about the modest tin-roofed Dominican farmhouses in the surrounding hills with elements from Oliver Messel's theatrical homes in the Caribbean—their zigzagging walkways and verandas built around big old trees, the whimsical pavilions and lagoon-like pools.

In this spirit, my team and I dreamed up the lattice cabanas by the swimming pool and a bar in the clubhouse inlaid with shells. We designed columns topped with copper palm fronds and iron chandeliers that resemble swimming octopi. In the dining room, a pair of antique striped canvas cabanas give the room the fanciful air of *Mary Poppins.* My hope was to inspire and spark the imagination. To take you out of the rush and grind of daily life, and encourage the soul to take flight.

My friend Juan Alberto, chef/owner of the wonderful restaurant El
Babunuco in the hills of Cabrera, gave me his collection of vintage
Dominican hand-knotted fishing nets when I marveled at their
astonishing intricacy. And they soon became the inspiration for the
front gates of the property. Constructed of thousands of feet of
fishing line, they came together in an ethereal gossamer weave that
sets the tone for the playful, dreamlike nature of the resort itself.
Here, even the metalwork has ruffles, and the gates are meant to
collect free spirits, much like a net gathers fish.

The swimming pool is the heart of Playa Grande. So many afternoons have been whiled away here, watching my kids go between the beach and the cabanas and the clubhouse, then tear back across the lawn and cannonball into the pool. Dominican architect Sarah Garcia drew the fantastical vaulted lattice cabanas that, with their lightness and whimsy, tell visitors that playfulness is exalted.

The Old Age of Nostalgia

by Mark Strand

Those hours given over to basking in the glow of an imagined future, of being carried away in streams of promise by a love or a passion so strong that one felt altered forever and convinced that even the smallest particle of the surrounding world was charged with purpose of impossible grandeur; ah, yes, and one would look up into the trees and be thrilled by the wind-loosened river of pale, gold foliage cascading down and by the high, melodious singing of countless birds; those moments, so many and so long ago, still come back, but briefly, like fireflies in the perfumed heat of a summer night.

I love the touch of pastoral lightheartedness these vintage English sheep statues bring to the lawn at Playa Grande. They announce that you're in a dream space—a place where all kinds of strange, wonderful things are possible.

The stone lions came from a favorite vintage collector, Bruce Erhard, on Dixie Highway in West Palm Beach. They're quite grand, but my fantasy is that instead of standing imperiously on guard, they are magical, welcoming creatures who announce that you're in an enchanted kingdom—a place for dreaming. With their chins lifted, they sing out to the jungle and the palm trees and the ocean, facing both ways to assert that there is neither an in nor an out in mind.

I love the idea of water dripping down like flower nectar to wash off your feet. Few objects are merely functional at Playa Grande. Even the plumbing creeps like a vine. And the bungalows themselves were all built around the great trees. Our rule was: If a trunk is more than ten inches in diameter, build around it. Nothing makes me happier than seeing a palm tree shooting up through an arbor, or a roofline that gives way to a tree.

For the *bahia* (the traditional Taino Indian word for "communal meeting place"), my fantasy was tied into the beauty of decaying formality. Stately decorative elements like wall brackets, which would normally hold fancy pottery, are shell-encrusted and instead carry dilapidated processional relics from an old church in Mexico. Similarly, the vintage ottoman's bullion fringe has messy hair, and I like it that way. Everything has a degree of finish, but the finish has gone feral.

Some of my happiest times in college were spent lolling around the dining hall over breakfast, in conversations so interesting that they continued into lunch. I wanted to create a similar atmosphere in the *bahia*—an open, welcoming place where people could come and go throughout the day for meals and talk and laughter and cocktails. The thirty-foot pale aqua ceiling and Italian gessoed shell chairs from Princess Sybil of Bourbon-Parma tell you that this is a place for dreaming and appreciation. The alien octopi chandeliers and the papier-mâché lionfish Carnival mask above the mirror remind us that there is no true beauty without a few beasts!

Nothing is more restful than reading a book while swinging on a daybed—especially when you can hear the ocean crashing in the distance. At any beach house, you want to create as many spaces for idling and dreaming as possible. The sea invites us to meditate and imagine. A good beach house enables and encourages us to accept this invitation.

"Fantasy is a necessary ingredient in living. It's a way of
looking at life through the wrong end of the telescope . . .
and that enables you to laugh at life's realities."
—Dr. Seuss

Wicker, to me, is the most light-stepping of all furniture. It almost tiptoes through a room, and because it can be woven into such beautiful forms, you often find it making fanciful gestures that seem to encapsulate the spirit of the space itself.

This console grabbed me at a furniture fair and insisted I buy it—though at the time I had no idea where it might land. It's a funny sideshow of a piece: part table, part theater curtain, with oversize carved wooden tassels. The egrets above it are a reproduction of an Audubon print, and the table itself holds all kinds of strange treasures that I collected over the years on various beach walks and at flea markets: bottles covered in barnacles and snail shells and metal flowers. As with the vintage yellow enamel teapot and the 1970s palm tree glasses I found on eBay, or the tree snail shell found in the jungle that inspired a drawerpull, the only unifying factor was that my soul said yes when I saw them. If you pay attention to what delights you, you will not go wrong.

From here, you can see Punta Preciosa off in the distance. I never tire of standing on this beach—the bright whiff of the salt air, the low golden flash of the wet sand as the sea draws back and regathers itself. Most of the things I love remind me of nature. The sight of vintage sconces that look like tulips thrills me. A chair and sideboard covered in scallop shells remind me of a sailor's valentine—and sailor's valentines make me happy. It's that simple.

In the changing room at the pool bathhouse, there's always a bit of sand
on the tiled floor, always the smell of sunblock and the soothing splash of
someone showering off after a swim—or surf—in the ocean.

A tête-à-tête is a fantasy conversation alluded to in wicker.
It's the dream of sitting on a wave of sea-foam at cocktail
hour, talking to your favorite person. One sees in and one
sees out, and perhaps there are some stolen kisses . . .

My childhood bed in Florida was wrapped in iron vines, and it was the most delightful thing to look at when I woke up. With the help of Puerto Plata's master metalworker Neno (who custom made all of the incredible ironwork on the property), I went a little crazier in the master bedroom at my family's bungalow here, Casa Guava, turning the whole canopy into a wild chandelier with tiny lights tucked into the leaves. Small reading lamps bent like tulips hang over the headboard, and the bedside tables are swiveling lily pads, just big enough for a book and a glass of water.

Let there be sand dollars over the doorways! Let the vines twist a monstropolous sky!

There are all kinds of fantasy concoctions mixed in with the historic
Victorian carved woodwork: squiggly sunbursts and clover, tulips and
star flares. The sand dollar transom is one of our more modest creations.
Architectural preservationist Elric Endersby was instrumental in inspiring
and drawing our hand-carved elements.

I wanted the bed to feel like a daybed hanging from the trees in the jungle,
and then I thought: Why not let the canopy vines twist into a light fixture
in the ceiling?

FOLLOWING PAGES

If any image could capture a moment I dreamed of while I was designing
Playa Grande, it's this one: the sight of my own sand flea bedbunnies
jumping in a bed that's also a garden. Of course, the antique Victorian
circus tent takes the whole thing right over the top, and that's kind of the
point. This is a dream space, and dreams like to get a bit wild.

Light
Salt
Air

One of the great things about building a house by the ocean is that nature has already done much of the work for you. You're there, presumably, because you like the clear pouring sunlight and the thrashing green sea and the soft salty air. You like a bit of sand on your feet when you walk to lunch. You want these things to be a part of your life.

Certainly this was the case for me at Playa Grande. As I was designing, I thought often about how open our house in Palm Beach was when I was growing up—how many big windows and folding doors and porches it had, and how nice it was that there were no walls or hedges around the property separating us from the rest of the world. I thought about how all that fresh air carried with it the smell of gardenias growing outside or the quibbling of the wild parrots as they roosted in the trees. My dreams for Playa Grande were similar: to bring as many of the outside elements in as possible.

With this in mind, all discussions (be they about landscaping, decorating, or architecture) were centered around designing flowing, inclusive spaces that offered up views of the sea and the pool and the jungle. There is no "front" or "back" to the property, no one way through. Instead there are gingerbread-decked verandas and folding plantation shutters that turn living rooms into porches, lacy *tragaluz* transoms above the windows and doorways to let in sunlight and breezes, and long trellised gazebos around the swimming pool. Even the weathered copper front "gate" at the clubhouse entrance is a gate only in the most decorative sense. Inspired by a local hand-knotted fishing net, it's almost entirely permeable—all air and light. Really, the whole resort is like this. The idea was to encourage people to bask and dream and frolic. To go skinny-dipping at midnight and feel the grass between their toes.

If you're lucky enough to have a place that looks out to sea, you want to find as many ways to frame that view as you can. With the pool (which is at the center of our property on Playa Grande), I liked the idea of creating continuity with the ocean and the jungle, so when you stepped into the pool, you'd think: *Am I dipping my toe in water, or looking out to the edge of the world?*

Lattice cabanas provide the airiest of architecture in
the garden, offering shade from the relentless sun and
cover from passing showers.

My family's house, Casa Guava, was inspired by my great-grandparents' Victorian kit house, Duck's Nest, in Palm Beach, which also has a triple-gabled roof and a wraparound veranda. But I gave our house a more rustic feel by sheathing it in whitewashed, reclaimed *tabla de palma* and trimming it with hand-cut gingerbread and *tragaluz* wood cuttings that let light and air in over the windows and doors. By working with weathered, handcrafted materials and inviting the elements in whenever possible, I could create a looser kind of "jungle Victorian" sensibility that feels at home in the Dominican Republic.

Here again, at Casa Guava's little guesthouse, is the idea of permeability—of creating rooms in constant dialogue with the sea and the jungle. What looks like a living room wall is actually a series of hinged plantation shutters that fold back and transform the space into an airy open porch. The furniture is convertible, too: the light vintage rattan Paul Frankl seats can easily be pushed together into love seats or broken up into a circle if friends drop by for cocktails.

A hidden layer of glass in the wooden fretwork allows
light to flow into the room even if the doors are closed
and the air-conditioning is on. But most often, doors
are left open to welcome breezes and provide sightlines
out to the gardens and beach.

I framed pale, hand-painted Chinese tea paper depicting various flowers and placed it throughout the houses at Playa Grande. Technically, it's wallpaper, but it's so beautiful and airy, it looked like art to me. The giant ginger flower in the center is one of the fabulous monsters that grow in our gardens. It's so fleshy and complex, you almost expect it to talk.

LEFT AND BELOW:

Our favorite beach dog, Paloma, loves to nap on the cool porch tiles, while we humans tend to favor the hammocks for afternoon reading and rocking in the breeze.

Some things feel meant to be. This desk originally came from my childhood home in Florida, but it spent years keeping me company in my post-college apartment on Bedford Street in the West Village. Several houses later, I realized that it belonged at Playa Grande, and the cutout trim on the base became a motif that appears all over the resort. In the tea-paper painting above, the bromeliad flowers remind me of the Florida tropics, as does the vintage wicker chair, which probably came from somebody's beach resort in the 1940s.

The whole guesthouse can become a big bedroom (or living room or porch), depending on what you do with the shuttered doors. There are five sets of them in the master bedroom, so all the walls except one can be opened up. Here, too, the light pours in through the *tragaluz* fretwork above the doors and throws lovely patterned shadows across the floors.

Two layers of doors in ice cream colors (one with plantation shutters, one with glass) provide maximum options for air flow, privacy, and shade. When it's hot, we fling them all open, and when it's *really* hot, we close the glass doors and crank up the AC. Once again, the idea of permeability comes into play with the headboard, which is just a tracery iron frame upholstered in raffia.

Sometimes it's nice to switch a room up a bit. On a day when the red torch ginger flowers in our garden were looking particularly irresistible, I put some in a vase and echoed them with big poppy-red linen Euro shams on the bed. It's good to remember how easily the mood of a room can be shifted when you feel like it.

I designed this tile (pet name: Spinach Flower) to revel in the jagged interplay of vines and leaves and branches around us at Playa Grande. I love how they crawl up the shower wall and how leaves from the garden in little glass wall-vases echo them, too. I'm always thinking about how to sing the jungle back to itself.

From
Forty Little Polliwogs
by Anonymous

Forty little polliwogs
Swimming in a ditch,
Each so near alike,
They don't know which is which.

You can smell the ocean everywhere here.
You carry it in your hair.

Ode to Enchanted Light

by Pablo Neruda
Translated by Mark Strand

The light under the trees,
the light from high heaven.
The green
arbor
light
that flashes
in the leaf
and falls like fresh
white sand.

A grasshopper lifts
its sawing sound
over the clearness.

The world
is a full glass
of water.

I wanted this living room to feel like a garden, so I filled it with potted palms, figs, and elephant ears and hung botanical prints on the walls. Plenty of empty vessels also abound because we all love to bring flowers back from our walks.

RIGHT

The jagged edges of copper leaves throw tropical shadows on the floors, and columns erupt in festive sprays of palm fronds.

ABOVE AND OPPOSITE

Every beach house needs a place by the front door to throw sun hats and towels. As for the lady in the portrait above the antique wicker chairs, I love wondering about her interesting past.

FOLLOWING PAGES

In the dining room at Casa Guava, it's all about open doors and framing the garden. The whimsical iron chairs look light as air, more gestures than furniture, curling like vines around the table.

Kitchen Song

by Kimberly Cutter

Sing me a song of the simple kitchen

Sing me a song of the jungle life

Sing me the moon and

The monkey who stole it.

Sing me to sleep to-night !

From

The Walrus and the Carpenter
by Lewis Carroll

'O Oysters, come and walk with us!'
    The Walrus did beseech.
A pleasant walk, a pleasant talk,
    Along the briny beach:
'We cannot do with more than four,
    To give a hand to each.'

The eldest Oyster looked at him,
    But never a word he said:
The eldest Oyster winked his eye,
    And shook his heavy head —
Meaning to say he did not choose
    To leave the oyster-bed.

But four young Oysters hurried up,
    All eager for the treat:
Their coats were brushed, their faces washed,
    Their shoes were clean and neat —
And this was odd, because, you know,
    They hadn't any feet.

"The cure for anything is salt water:
sweat, tears or the sea."

—Isak Dinesen

PREVIOUS PAGES

This is a wonderful occasional dining room or sun porch inspired by my childhood bedroom in Palm Beach, which was originally a gazebo. Nothing is better than a high cathedral ceiling, with sun pouring in from all sides.

BELOW

There's nothing like the sweet taste of a freshwater outdoor shower after a long day on the beach. In theory, we installed it so you can rinse the sand off your feet, but really it's about drinking the fresh water after all the salt.

From
The Idea of Order at Key West
by Wallace Stevens

She sang beyond the genius of the sea.
The water never formed to mind or voice,
Like a body wholly body, fluttering
Its empty sleeves; and yet its mimic motion
Made constant cry, caused constantly a cry,
That was not ours although we understood,
Inhuman, of the veritable ocean.

In
the
Jungle

I grew up surrounded by a tuft of jungle in the 1970s, but wild acres in Palm Beach are very different from mountainous rainforest in the Caribbean. The Dominican landscape has real drama, from the snowcapped mountain of Pico Duarte to the limestone ocean cliffs on the north coast and the desert dunes of Baní. The colors are hotter, the shade is deeper, the plants are bigger and stranger. Some of the insects look big enough to harness. When you build and landscape in the islands, it's always with the knowledge that nature is in charge. You may have your fantasy of cultivation, but there's also a constant sense of barely restrained chaos waiting in the wings; and I like that tension. There's a dance you can do between wildness and civility, drawing power from the jungle's primordial magic while maintaining enough order and decorum to create a beautiful living space.

You want a lawn where your kids can play, and where you can lie out on chaises under the stars at night. You want a pool. You want lighted pathways.

But you don't want to kill the wild spirit that drew you there in the first place. My feeling is, if you're in the tropics and something doesn't bite you or burn you or sting you or get you wet sometimes, you've probably missed a lot.

So as my team and I worked, the challenge was to restrain the jungle where necessary and invite it in whenever possible. We commissioned iron canopy beds with vines that wind all over the ceiling and oxidized copper outdoor shower heads shaped like giant nodding flowers. Palm frond light fixtures cast a fringed glow in the library. Pierced copper star lanterns pay homage to the tropical sky. When it came to landscaping, our goal was to make gardens that felt like the jungle itself, and to carve delicate paths through the greenery, instead of destroying it. We knew the natural beauty surrounding the houses would be more important than what was inside them, but the idea was to reference the jungle so often in our design that it would all come to feel seamless. Like a glorious overgrown garden. With some heirloom china. And soft down pillows.

PAGE 117

This is a side entrance to Playa Grande as viewed from one of several pathways around the property that lead into the jungle. The idea was to contain the wilderness a bit as you approach the gates by planting ferns and palms and figs in big shell-and-earthenware pots along the mossy coquina stone path—indicating that you are now entering a space where the jungle will be celebrated but also cultivated.

PREVIOUS PAGES

"She is delightfully chaotic; a beautiful mess. Loving her is a splendid adventure." Author Steve Maraboli wrote those lines, but whenever I read them, I find myself thinking of this house, which contains both the communal library and the Star Bar at Playa Grande. It's surrounded on three sides by jungle, and offers one of the more potent combinations of refinement and wildness on the property. Going there always feels a little like entering the jungle itself—plus books and cocktails!

LEFT

For the library, I had a fantasy of the jungle as the place where the world traveler finds herself. It's an assemblage of treasures I collected during my own travels: Balinese ikats and batiks, Uzbek embroidery, African wax prints, and throw pillows made from old kilims. The wonderful Dutch portraits were collected by neighboring hotelier Marie-Claude Thiebault, and depict the ship captains and explorers I imagined as some of the library's early inhabitants. You see elements of "their" various collections around the room: odd vintage taxidermied birds under a bell jar, petrified shells on black paper, a giant puffer fish, a leather-and-wood toy carousel from nineteenth-century Paris. I painted the rattan a lovely plum color to pull the room together and give it a bit of glossy sophistication.

"The library is inhabited by spirits that come out of the pages at night."

—Isabel Allende

Playa Grande

Lyrics by SOFI TUKKER & Bomba Estéreo

We're gonna have a party

I'm gonna dance until my shoes ask me to stop

So I start to take off my shoes

Dance until I'm bruised

And all my clothes fall off

RIGHT

The Star Bar is a fabulous hodgepodge of oddities collected over the years. It's full of Indonesian ikat fabrics and swirls of pencil rattan with vintage tramp art cigar tables made of bottle caps. Nearby hang fishing nets and Australian Aboriginal paintings, with a Polaroid of Truman Capote thrown in for good measure. In my fantasy, while the serious world travelers are reading downstairs, the more decadent ones are up here, drinking tequila and howling at the night sky on the balcony.

Many of the books in the library came from my stepmother's collection. She works in a bookstore, so it includes a lot of galley proofs, combined with beach reads and classics and super-academic texts from some of our more illustrious guests. We have a take-a-book, leave-a-book policy, so you'll find everything here, from Jackie Collins to Isak Dinesen to Proust. The wonderfully fussy (but also somehow primitive) antique wicker chair has so much personality, I half expect it to trot upstairs when no one is watching and dance in the light of the star chandelier.

The wonderful thing about the jungle is that it contains so many different elements and creatures—from ants to mushrooms to flowers the size of dinner plates to ominous birds of prey—and yet, somehow, it's all held together by the great green webs of branches and vine. At Playa Grande, the unifying design element (or web, if you will) was love. I let myself go out and gather all kinds of different textures and fabrics and treasures and creatures that I loved, things that felt like they belonged there. Then I let the place itself tell me what to do with them—which piece belonged where, and which other things it wanted to be friends with. It's a kind of listening, the way I design. If you pay enough attention to a place, it will tell you what it needs, and if you pay enough attention to each thing, it will tell you where it belongs.

Elephants trumpet, vines twist, palm
fronds spray from the ceiling…it's the
idea of letting the jungle take over a bit,
letting it weave its way into your life.

"Everybody who's anybody longs to be a tree."

—Rita Dove

When your head is really in the jungle, you realize that palm fronds are uniquely elegant conveyers of light, and even your one-inch copper water pipe could become a vine that wove itself around a tree. The shower is open, the wild sky stretches itself out overhead, and the wood planks are warm under your feet—this is the dream of island life.

RIGHT

The jungle is the best partner in creating privacy. Big potted palms bring shade and enclosure to the porches, while coral pavers dropped irregularly along the low, tight grass make a playful hopscotch grid that wanders and meanders through the overgrowth, infusing even the walk to breakfast or a dash back to the bungalow to grab a hair tie with a sense of exploration.

FOLLOWING PAGES

In this guesthouse, the woody browns of the jungle play off a white background, creating a spare, clean frame for the wild profusion of greenery just outside. I used grain sacks and kilims from the Anatolian plateau to make pillows, and brought in more of Paul Frankl's convertible rattan to allow for a multitude of seating arrangements. When all the doors are folded back, this room feels like a lovely floating ice cube in the middle of the rainforest.

PREVIOUS PAGES

Let the paint peel on the ironwork; let the world have its way a bit. See what nature does with your ideas of order and control. Let there be a dance between beauty and the inevitable decay.

RIGHT

In this guesthouse, the dark woven vintage wicker furniture stands out against the glossy white floors and crisp white woodwork. There's a lovely tension between primitive and refined, light and dark.

I had the ceiling above the *tragaluz* woodwork in this bungalow candy-caned in yellow and white and then I had all the fan paddles wrapped in wicker. The idea was to conjure a sense of play wherever possible, to keep the dance of wildness and civility alive at every turn.

Beauty is everywhere. Even a grouping of humble vintage stove burner grates can make for playful decor in the right setting. Here, the black iron starbursts add a graphic pop to the white wall and serve as a kind of inside-out echo of the black-and-white *tragaluz* cutouts in the ceiling.

The flowers get positively Jurassic here. They're not fragile at all. They're fleshy and flamboyant—part flower, part dragon. Our favorite tropical flowers (like the bromeliads at right) appear on hand-painted Chinese tea paper framed in *tabla de palma* in each of the bungalows.

"I always put in one controversial item.
It makes people talk."
—Dorothy Draper

The brilliant ironworkers at Neno Industrial in Puerto Plata, most of them Neno's family members, made this bathroom into a jungle all its own, complete with an oxidized star-flower-vine mirror, a giant flower sink basin, and a little matching flower-petal table.

THESE PAGES

The sway and curl of tropical flowers becomes geometry in custom concrete tile, while the black-and-white palette echoes the intense play of sun and shadow found in the jungle. An antique wicker chair coils itself tightly all over in homage to fiddlehead ferns.

FOLLOWING PAGES

One of the prettiest sights in the world is the Star Bar emerging like a glowing ocean liner at the edge of the jungle as you walk toward it for a drink after dinner. Sometimes we'll turn the music up loud and come back out and dance in the grass. Sometimes I just stand there staring at the spectacle and hoping the night never ends.

Sweet

&

Dark

There were a lot of salt-faded bathing suits and men's espadrilles in lavender and lemon and coral roaming around in my 1970s Palm Beach childhood, and I've been inspired by those slightly off-kilter pastels ever since. The more worn-in they get, the better they look (which is good in the tropics, where the sun is always waiting to sink its teeth into them). Also, if you think of a coastal home as a natural extension of the beach and sky, it makes sense that the Creamsicle clouds and the pale, wavy green glass of the sea would want to come inside.

So I knew early on that the houses at Playa Grande would have whitewashed exteriors with pastel accents: ceilings the weathered blue of an old surfer's eyes, and trims the yellow of good French butter. I knew there would be floral tablecloths and posies on the sheets, headboards the shade of freshly sliced cucumbers, tiles painted to match a handful of shells. What I didn't expect was the herd of fierce, almost primal colors that would soon insist on joining the party.

It was the jungle knocking, of course. As a rule of thumb, the dominant colors you see in the natural landscape around you will always work happily inside. And because the colors of the surrounding rainforest at Playa Grande are bold, it turned out I could get away with all kinds of surprising combinations in the houses. I found myself drawn to African wax prints in swirling Gauguin shades like fuchsia and malachite, blood red and aged Gouda. In came a lacquered raspberry bureau and lamps painted Yves Klein's über-pigmented blue. Up marched black lacquer cane chairs with squid-ink-and-white African batik cushions. Behind came matching batik canopies and wicker headboards the deep dusky green of forest shade.

As I'd hoped, these beastie colors sang thrillingly together against the white and pastel backdrop, bringing the rooms to life in a way I couldn't have expected. And once I dipped my toe into the African wax prints, the floodgates were open. I realized that a lot of the wilder textiles I'd fallen in love with and collected during my travels over the years—from Uzbek ikats and antique embroidery to Indonesian batiks to woven cape trims from Burma—would work here. Not only would they work, they'd be the special sauce. What I found is that these heartier elements—often dyed and woven by hand—created a language with the delicate macaron colors of Palm Beach that felt both authentic and fresh. They brought a much-needed element of drama and irony to the space, throwing a shriek and a belly laugh in to balance out all the sweetness. It was a good lesson. And in a way, it's always the same lesson: *Go with what you love. If you love it, it will work.*

There's nothing nicer than retreating into the cool shade of a bungalow after a hot, sweaty day on the beach. The Caribbean sun can get intense, and there's a point each afternoon when you need to escape its beady-white glare and the high-pitched whine of the cicadas. At such times, deep covered porches and breezy interiors become a delicious haven for napping and reading.

Tropic Winter
by Evelyn Scott

The afternoon is frozen with memories,
Radiant as ice.
The sun sets amidst the agued trembling of the leaves;
Sinking right down through the gold air
Into the arms of the sea.
And the enameled wings of the palm trees
Keep shivering, shivering
Beating the old air thin...

It's not all fruits and flowers. The sweetness of melon-and-mint-colored tiles balances well with a touch of voodoo color and macabre decoupage art.

Fierce Carnival masks of octopi and coral monstrosities offset the gentle sand and seashell tones of a comfortable sitting room. I had the pillows made out of cotton rag rugs, and the kids brought the coconuts in from a beach walk.

Vintage 1950s shirt collars and neckties provide a dark yet hopeful reminder of a Willy Loman–like persona. Just as the Carnival masks remind us of our more savage sides, these old-school neckties point to the fact that any businessman's buttoned-up self is also just a role he has elected to play in his "real" life—one that can and should be set aside as soon as he sets foot in a beach house.

Homemade granola with fresh cantaloupe and local honey is one of my favorite breakfasts at Playa Grande . . . though my *real* favorite is French toast topped with powdered sugar and rhubarb compote! And then, of course, there is my other favorite . . . avocado splayed on fried queso fresco.

A soothing backdrop of white walls and tutu-pink trim is brought to life by furniture in deep jungle colors like bloody raspberry and taxicab yellow, while the ocean gets a nod from a pair of lamps the electric blue of a betta fish. Simple vintage straw trivets splash similar hot colors on the walls and create an ideal balance between sweet and dark.

The gentle face and sharp teeth of a green Rajasthani lion-dog (made of vintage sari fabric) make for a great playful monster in a kid's bedroom, while a cream, pink, ochre, and eggplant dhurrie does a happy dance with African batiks the colors of exotic fruits.

Hot mango-colored modern abstract art captures the
chaotic spirit of jungle flowers, while silver-and-bamboo
barware adds the debonair nature of cocktail hour.

In the evenings at nearby Laguna Gri-Gri, where a river of dark water flows through the mangrove roots to the ocean, hundreds of white egrets come to roost, squawking and swooping into their nests as the sun goes down. Nothing is more fun than passing through these mangroves on skiffs and laughing at whoever gets pooped on by the vultures in the trees far above.

"In order for the light to shine so brightly,
the darkness must be present."

—Francis Bacon

In the foyer, the colors of sunset and late-day shade in this
piece of Brutalist art pick up the tones of beautifully decayed
sea grape leaves, barnacles, and flowers in vitrines on the
console. On the floor, a dyed-goat-hair kilim brings just the
right amount of shadow inside.

The Coming of Light

by Mark Strand

Even this late it happens:
the coming of love, the coming of light.
You wake and the candles are lit as if by themselves,
stars gather, dreams pour into your pillows,
sending up warm bouquets of air.
Even this late the bones of the body shine
and tomorrow's dust flares into breath.

People never think of leaves falling in the tropics, but they do, and it's gorgeous, especially the almond leaves, which decay into a verdant rust color. I mimicked those leaves with fanciful Mexican pom-poms, making a dreamy tangle over the beds in a kids' room, as well as letting beautifully decrepit metal flowers on the bedside table bear further witness to the passage of time.

In this guest room, I started out with a bold array of African wax print fabrics and put them all in a boxing ring together. The ones left standing were the ones that balanced each other in the most interesting ways. The trick, when you work with intense colors like these, is to add in some shades that serve as neutrals and temper the heat. Here, African batiks in squid ink and white work alongside geometric charcoal-and-white bed skirts and dark green wicker headboards to keep the room from boiling over!

Bravely goes the fierce rock
lobster, sweetly sighs the
wicker afternoon.

Texture

Texture is the secret weapon of any great beach house. It's the pleasing roughness of sun-warmed stone as you get out of the swimming pool, the silky coolness of concrete tiles underfoot as you head to cocktails. It's the frayed edge of an antique life preserver so weathered it's a piece of sculpture, the weave of a crocheted hammock as you settle in for an afternoon nap. (I'm specifically *not* referencing the bumpy crisscrossed pattern you find scored into your bottom after that nap.)

Tactile elements like these may seem minor, but they're essential to creating a space that elates and comforts. Textures settle people into their bodies and focus their senses in a way little else can. So when it came to choosing materials for Playa Grande, I thought a lot with my fingers and feet and backside. (How does this fabric feel beneath my thighs? The back of this chair against my spine?) You want to find textures that draw you in, that soothe or intrigue or delight. It's these subtle sensory aspects of houses (especially vacation houses) that people remember—the things that etch themselves into the memories of the ones you love and entice them to come back year after year.

At Playa Grande, many of the textures I used evoke nostalgia because they were purchased in a moment of passion while I was traveling, or because they reminded me of some particularly tasty summer day from my childhood. I chose rough porous coralina stone to hopscotch the walking paths that wind through our property and frame the pool because it reminded me of the coral stone pavers that connected my family's house in Palm Beach to my grandparents' house when I was a kid. Similarly, memories of "ice-skating" across my mother's sunporch floor in socks inspired me to have the sun-bleached ipe floors on the verandas sanded until they were so smooth you could glide across them. (Did I secretly hope that one day I'd find my own kids doing the same thing I used to? I did.)

Emotions matter when you're creating a home. Notice the handwoven linen kilim that reminds you of a hairy coconut, which reminds you of the palm tree where you had your first kiss. Notice how a hooded wicker armchair makes you feel like Daisy Buchanan in *The Great Gatsby.* Choose the grass that resembles the lawn where you learned to do a cartwheel or first played Duck-Duck-Goose. Find ways to weave these lovely, subtle reminders of your life—and the things you love most about it—into your beach house and you will find you've made a haven no one ever wants to leave.

PAGE 200

I spent a lot of time collecting shells on beach walks with my mother when I was a child, so they have a special place in my heart. In the *bahia*, my team and I pressed shells—some real, some handmade of patinated copper—into a kind of oceanic rainbow around the bar. I've never met a beach house that wasn't improved by the speckled and intricately formed presence of some shells—especially when they've been gathered by guests and family members.

LEFT

The gorgeous sculptural coral stone cliffs that rise above and around the jungle at Playa Grande thrill me anew each time I see them. To walk barefoot here is to know the feel of that rough, sun-warmed stone beneath your feet, to see the ocean's wavy blue chop rolling out around you and the jungle trees reaching their wild arms to the sky.

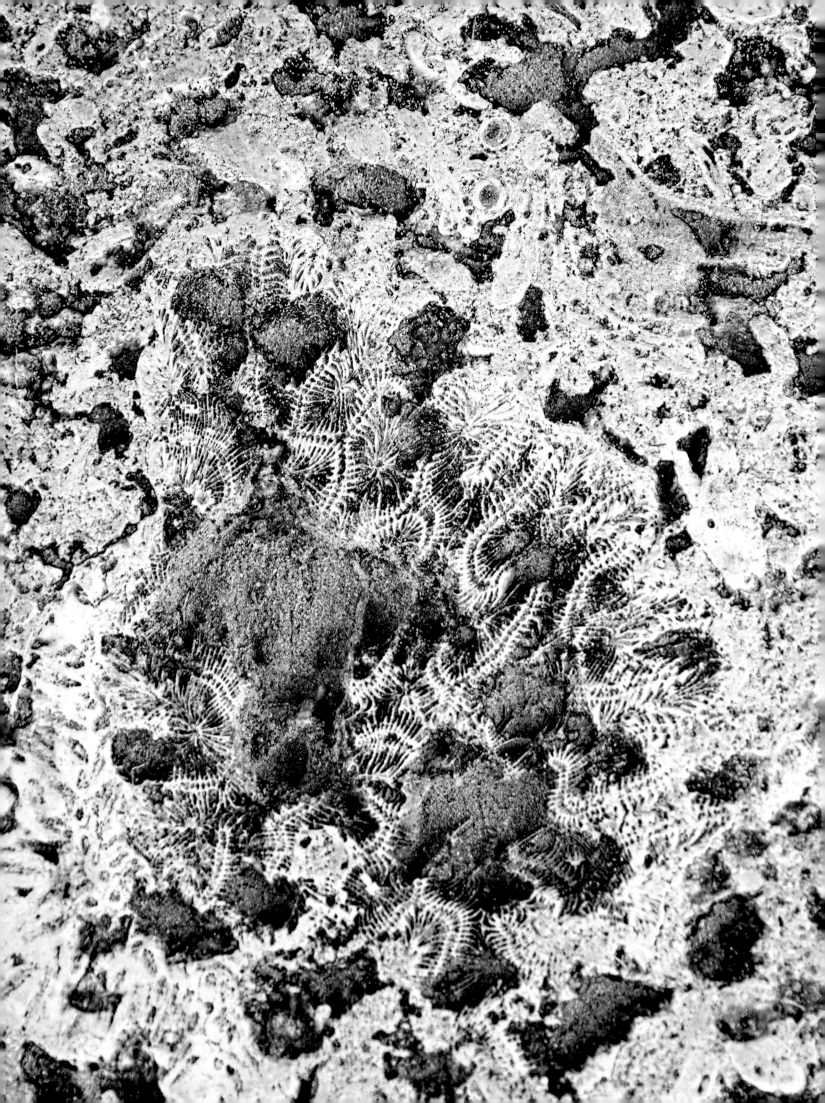

One of my favorite words is "be-lichened," and the mossy growth on the porous coral stone pavers around the pool is a great example. The soft black-green mulch of mossy swirls appears inside patterns made by fossilized shell forms. Meanwhile, in the cabanas, delicate fronds of coral are echoed in the trellis architecture and the webbing of 1970s spun resin furniture. We helped the vines grow up from the ground outside and crawl in through the ceiling for a true celebration of the jungle, topped off with a woven cane chandelier built to resemble big palm nut blooms.

It's impossible to discuss texture without talking about the texture of the air around Playa Grande—the laughter and shouts and giggles of children and the flirtations of teenagers swimming at Laguna Gri-Gri in nearby Rio San Juan, the eternal hum of birds and bugs and mopeds, the juicy jangle of merengue and bachata music, the occasional thumping of Nicki Minaj. That's the texture of life here. We're layered into the countryside on the north coast, among coconut palms and cattle pastures between two small towns, and I like to think that all of those things inspired me when I was designing the resort—that it wasn't just the natural beauty but also the vibrant culture and overall gusto of my Dominican friends.

A home is not simply a building; it is the shelter around the intimacy of a life. Coming in from the outside world and its rasp of force and usage, you relax and allow yourself to be who you are. The inner walls of a home are threaded with the textures of one's soul, a subtle weave of presences. If you could see your home through the lens of the soul, you would be surprised at the beauty concealed in the memory your home holds. When you enter some homes, you sense how the memories have seeped to the surface, infusing the aura of the place and deepening the tone of its presence. Where love has lived, a house still holds the warmth. Even the poorest home feels like a nest if love and tenderness dwell there.

— John O'Donohue
from *Beauty: The Invisible Embrace*

"Up in this air you breathed easily, drawing in a vital assurance and lightness of heart ... you woke up in the morning and thought: Here I am, where I ought to be."

—Isak Dinesen

A local Dominican artist made the laser-cut gourd lanterns that hang from one of the verandas. I love to come here with a glass of lemonade in the afternoon after a long round of tennis.

Old playing cards and seashells painted on a vintage cane backgammon board will always feel wistful, playful, and handcrafted all at once. Next door, a woven wicker shade and a chunky mid-century California pottery lamp provide earthy ballast to an airy bedroom that otherwise might float away. With the smooth white crispness of Italian sheets and sheer linen curtains, oxidized copper bedside lights and twiggy bureau handles work to keep it all tethered to the ground.

Something as seemingly mundane as closet drawers for underwear
and bathing suits come to vibrant life when woven with wicker
tendrils and painted hot turquoise.

A snaking rope of shells and seaglass-like glassware suggests treasures found on a beach walk and also dresses up the dinner table without stuffy formality.

I've been collecting these rusty Spanish flower specimens in ceramic pots since I was in my twenties. Their swaying stems remind me of our towering palm trees at Playa Grande, and I like that their rust is as much a feature as their paint colors.

You'd think that a weird old hollowed-out wood carving of fighting cocks, combined with a crisp, finely carved, powder-blue-and-white sunburst of Dominican fretwork, on top of an antique mirror bar back, surrounded by a giant archway of shells, the bar itself, would be *way* too much, but somehow it all works together. (Not unlike the insane medley of rum, red wine, honey, tree bark, and herbs in the batch of Mamajuana aging in its jug behind Christian as he tends bar.) I can't tell you why, except to say that I loved all of these things, and I listened to them until they arranged themselves and coalesced into something essential.

OPPOSITE

More is more in the Star Bar. The whole thing is a carnival of texture and pattern. It's meant to overwhelm you with its cornucopia of vintage weaves and prints from various time periods and from all over the world, collected over years of travel. It's Dutch wax prints on top of Indonesian ikat on top of swirling 1960s pencil rattan on top of kilims. Aboriginal crafts and pieces of tramp art, like a cigar table made out of bottle caps, play off a hoe turned into a bird sculpture. By day, the room is vivid and colorful and patterned, and by night, it recedes into the darkness as the star lanterns come to life, freckling the walls and ceiling with light.

Sweet Heat

Serves 1

3 ounces tequila blanco
2 ounces fresh lime juice
1 ounce Poblano Chili Pepper Honey Syrup
    (see below)
Jalapeños, sliced thin, for garnish

Combine the tequila, lime juice, and syrup in a shaker with ice. Shake vigorously. Pour into a rocks glass over ice. Top with 2 or 3 thin slices of jalapeño.

POBLANO CHILI PEPPER HONEY SYRUP
1 cup dark honey
½ cup water
4 poblano chili peppers, sliced into thin coins
    (see note)

Combine the honey, water, and peppers in a pot and bring to a boil. Remove from the heat and let cool to room temperature.

Note: You can remove the seeds from the poblano chili peppers for less heat.

Tamarind Shandy

Serves 1

1 ounce Tamarind Simple Syrup (see below)
1 ounce fresh lime juice
1 (12-ounce) can of Presidente beer

Add the tamarind simple syrup to a highball glass. Add the lime juice. Finish with the Presidente.

TAMARIND SIMPLE SYRUP
⅓ cup (a little less than 3 ounces) tamarind
    concentrate
1 cup granulated sugar
1 cup water

Bring the tamarind concentrate, sugar, and water to a boil. Remove from the heat and let it cool to room temperature.

OPPOSITE

In the *bahia*, a color palette of whites, pastels, and natural, weathered wood helps unify the wild cacophony of textures. Many of the materials here are local—from the rough-hewn, chevronned *tabla de palma* on the bar, to the elegant hand-painted concrete floor tiles. All of them were things I loved, things that took me back to my slightly feral, quasi-Victorian childhood in Palm Beach or to my travels, or took me forward somehow, toward dreams I had for the future. It is this weave of loves—past, present, and future—that is essential when creating a home.

There are some textures machines can't reproduce. When you use handmade textiles, you can feel the weave, the individual handwork that went into making it. As in nature, variations and irregularities cause each piece to catch the light differently. Each is as unique as a fingerprint.

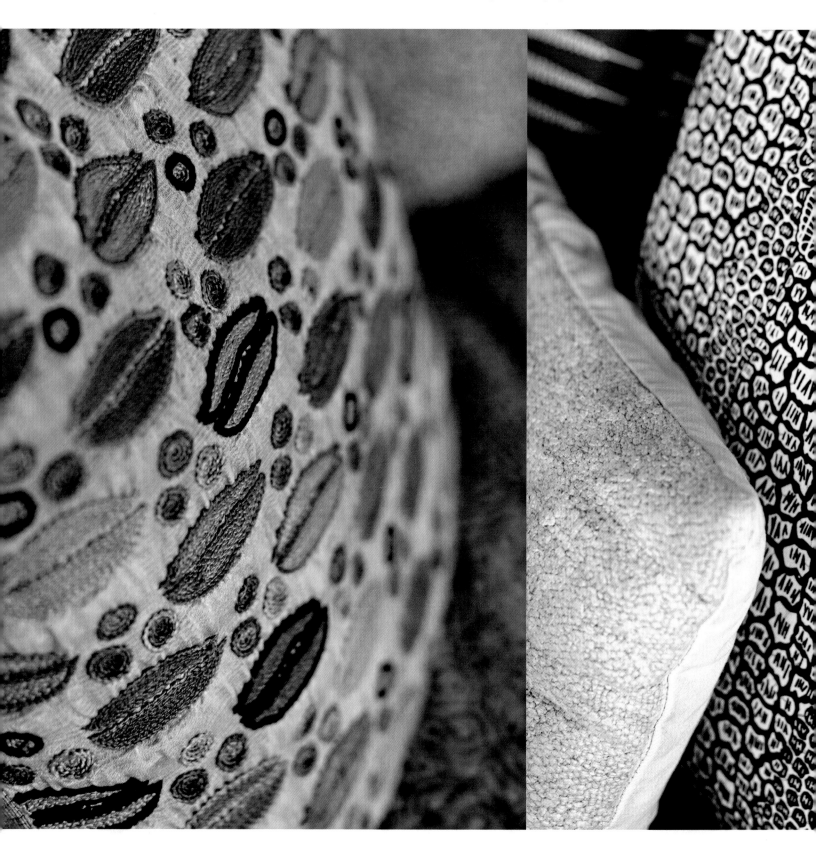

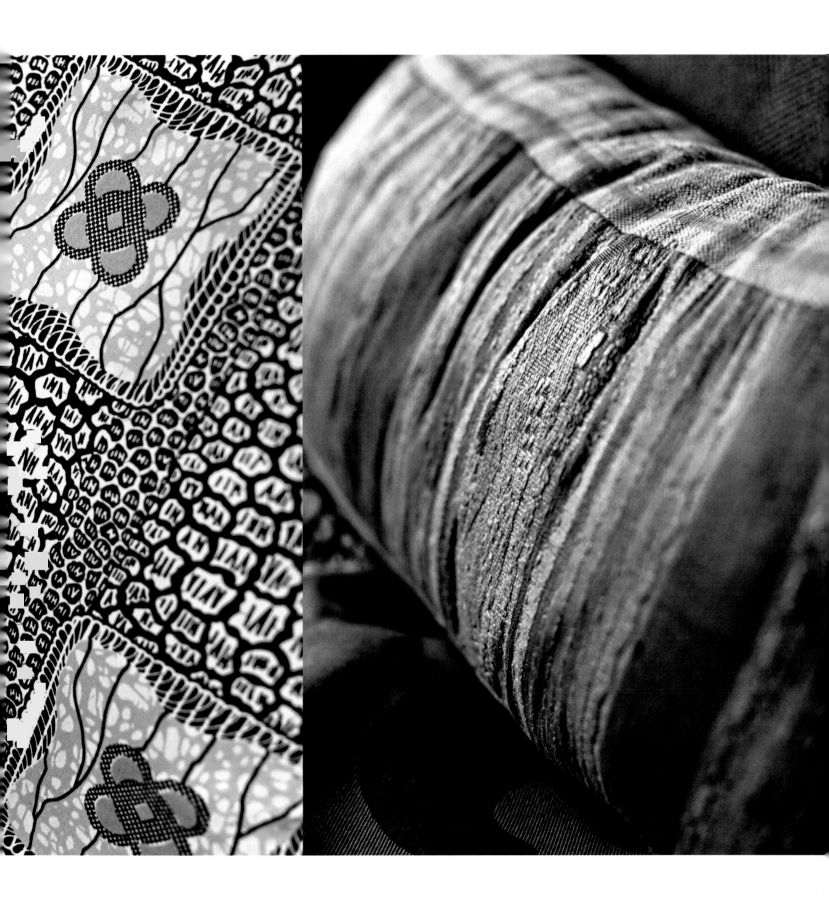

The Walk Back

These days, when I walk down the beach at sunset, I feel like I'm returning home. I catch sight of the lights of the club peeking out from the jungle, the pale aqua corrugated roofs catching the last of the sun as it slips into the West, and I know my people are there waiting for me—my kids probably still horsing around in the pool, my friends and family slowly gathering on the porch for cocktails with sunburnt shoulders and freshly showered hair.

In the years since we first came to Playa Grande, this beach has been the setting for more memories than I can count. I've known the joy of watching my children take their first wobbly steps toward the ocean (between sticking fistfuls of sand in their mouths) and of hearing them gasp in astonishment at the sight of humpbacks snarfing white fountains of water into the sky. I've had the thrill of drinking a cocktail at the shell-encrusted bar that once only existed in my imagination. I've heard the shrieks and helpless laughter of my mother upon discovering a land crab in her shower—claws raised for battle. I've known the awe of lying out on the lawn late at night with the palm trees arching overhead in black silhouette, watching the stars fall from millions of miles away, their gold lights blazing down around us.

In the end, it's memories like these that make a house into a home. The job of a designer, really, is to create spaces that will enable and inspire such memories. As I've said, good design is a marriage of self and setting, and it is this marriage you'll want to bear in mind if you find yourself designing a home by the beach. Keep coming back to your heart and the natural world around you as you work. It may sound cheesy or pat, but your heart will remind you of the things and people that matter most—who you really are—and the surrounding coastal landscape, with its natural beauty and harmonious palette, will show you the colors and textures, the patterns and objects that will thrive most happily there.

Whenever I got stuck while planning some design element at Playa Grande, I developed a habit of walking down the beach or hiking up into the jungle to clear my head. Each time, I'd set off feeling sure I'd never find a solution to whatever problem was dogging me. I'd be focused on the impasse, my vision clouded by frustration. But inevitably, as soon as I forgot about the problem and lost myself in my surroundings, a solution would appear, seemingly out of the blue. Sometimes, it was the fresh briny breeze whisking off the water, reminding me to keep finding new ways to invite that gorgeous air inside the houses. Other times, it was the wild green web of the jungle reminding me how many different elements and creatures (from fire ants to wine-cap mushrooms to orchids to birds of prey) can co-exist happily within a single space, as long as they're held together by a unifying design element, like vines. Or love.

Love your house enough, pay attention to it, and you'll be amazed at the magical thing it grows into. Keep adding things that remind you of your deepest dreams and your highest hopes, the ones that make you feel free and excited and a little bit glamorous, the ones that make you feel like a kid again.

Of course, nothing works out exactly the way you think it will. But if you allow your passion, your imagination, and your surroundings to guide you, the result will be deeply personal and authentic—a web of family and friendship, dreams and desire that is always growing and shifting, and always calling you home.

Acknowledgments

Of all the lessons Playa Grande has taught me, two in particular stand out. One is that there is very little in this life that we truly do on our own. The second is that the more people we involve and depend on and collaborate with, the more wonderful our lives are apt to become.

First, I want to thank Boykin, without whom the Playa Grande Beach Club would not exist. While this book is about the design only, the thank-you is for sharing in the complicated processes of dreaming, building, and being our family. To our children, Rascal, Zinnia, and Wick: you are the best wishes ever realized and the spark that animates all that we imagined. I am grateful for every day that I get to watch you become more and more yourselves.

Playa Grande has brought to the Curry, Kemble, and Kemble-Curry families years of learning, lots of hard work, occasional rest, and amazing joy and memories. I am grateful to Boykin, Beth, and Ravenel and our founding group for trusting me with the design of our houses and club. And to the group and those who served as advisers and contributors in other ways, thank you for what you shared and for the opportunity to get to know you and your families. Because there are so many of you to acknowledge, and with some privacy in mind, I'm using first names only (in no particular order): Carola, Bibi, Marisa, Mirtha, Andrew, Jon, Andy, Anne, John, Chris, Alice, Lela, Brandon, Jeff, Hailey, Steve, Mike, Sukey, Jonathan, Jennifer, Leslie, Bill, Geoff, Ginger, Fareed, Paula, John, Vadim, Vadim, Charlie, Graham, Courtney, Scott, Laura, John, Cary, Kathy, Mark, Roberto, Chris, Sherman, Marie, Mariska, Andrew, Peter, James, Richard, Spencer, Rebecca, Suzanne, Mark, Susannah, Antonio, Caroline, Rob, Marshall, Elizabeth, Gabrielle, Diedra, Joe, Daniel, Bryan, Marina, Jasmit, Chris, Pepe, Adrian, Bebe, Charlie, Ruben, Miguel Angel, Victoria, Vicky, Stuart, Jo Ann, John, Corky, KC, Josh, and Lauren.

I must also thank my family, Mimi and Leigh McMakin, Bill, Julie, Madeleine, and Phoebe, for standing by me and loving me through the years and years and years. You are the gravity and center to my sometimes wobbly and always expanding solar system.

Jenn Grandchamp was my eyes, hands, and design colleague most dedicated to the Playa Grande project—her fingerprints are on everything. Jenn, I will never forget that you got your first passport for this project and now, as a designer with such vast talent, the world is yours. I have loved working alongside you! Thanks always to the women of Kemble Interiors and their astounding collective creative firepower. Among them, special thanks go to Liza Morten Gioia, who has helped immeasurably with this book and has become the den mother and all-around Renaissance woman on our Kemble team.

Although my beloved friend Delio, to whom this book is dedicated, did not live to see Playa Grande reach completion, it was his infectious energy, optimism, and love of the Dominican Republic that helped launch the entire undertaking. Delio was always dancing. Not just at parties. Or on beaches. Delio knew that hard work is a dance. Relationships are, too. He taught me that to make things happen and to enjoy the process, you need to get others to dance with you.

It was the thought of Delio dancing—the way his joy lifted everybody up and made us want to be a part of whatever magic he was making—that showed me a way forward with Playa Grande. Thanks to him, I sensed that if I could let my passion lead me, I would be able to get great people in on the dance with me, and together, we could create something special. I never understood how true this was until I watched Playa Grande slowly but surely rise up out of the jungle at the hands of the incredible crew of builders and craftsmen and artists and designers and landscapers who came together to help create it.

Playa Grande Beach Club was realized as it was only because of the melded understanding of Caribbean architecture and Dominican spirit by the visionary and superbly tasteful builders Mark Johnson, Gary Hastings, Adolfo Ramirez, Roberto Ruiz, Fernando Solano, and Benny Martinez; landscape and site development by Whandy Martinez, Juan Diego Vasquez, and Hart Howerton; architectural consulting by Sarah Garcia and collaboration and poetic drawings by preservationist and mensch Elric Endersby; adept project management by Alicia Lalane, Franklin Angomás, Patricia Cedeño, Lliliany Gomez; and the work of key craftsmen: Nelson, Neno, Yellow, and Smiley.

Rolando Fernández de Castro, whom I have appointed as my Dominican godfather, really came before the beginning. He and Massiel García played so many different roles over the years that assigning any description to them seems limiting whereas my gratitude is infinite.

My friend Bronson van Wyck has stuck with me since we both fell in love with the same boy at fourteen. How we have grown—and not grown up—but also grown together! Bronson, thank you for being one of my great constants and a source of so much insight and adventure, especially on this one.

Stephen Roesler, thank you for every minute because when I am with you I am exactly where I want to be.

For time we've spent on the baseball field, on the skiffs, at the bar, by the bonfire, on horseback, on the courts and greens, eating the pig, and dancing—Christina, Al, Al, Becca, Margo, Neeta, Jeff, Will, Dan, Fred, Scott, Marzo, John, Chris, Kelynn, Emily, Paul, Sara, Justin, Rob, Caroline, Brody, and all my other friends who've helped me build a bigger web and new traditions here: I love you all.

Kim Cutter is always a best friend and in this instance was also my brilliant cowriter. She knows how precious this story, book, and place are to me and was essential in helping me find the words to express it. (She is also the only person I know who can write the poems of my dreams with one hand while grabbing me by the tail with the other.) Another wrangler of the impossible, Aliza Fogelson and I have now borne three books together! Without Aliza's imagination, diligence, patience, and excellence as an editor, I'd just have a desk full of sticky notes and a bedside table full of late-night scratchings. Michelle Cohen has made this book flow visually and brought refinement and warmth though her design. Charles Miers, Lynn Scrabis, Colin Hough Trapp, and the Rizzoli team, thank you for the opportunity to show a broader group something I feel so passionately about.

Photographer Karyn Millet went for a quick vacation and found herself and her husband completely shanghaied into a whirlwind of a photo shoot that turned into this book. Karyn, I know you did this because you fell in love with Playa Grande, and Dan, because you are an awesome husband and the best swim-trunks-wearing, impromptu photo assistant who isn't a photo assistant. Meg Connolly and team at Meg Connolly PR, thanks for seeing the work and heart behind Playa Grande and being inspired to jump on board and help us out.

For showing Playa Grande in such a beautiful light (figuratively and literally), thanks also go to photographers Francois Halard, Douglas Friedman, Patrick Cline, Pip Cowley, and Meghan Mehan; Carlos Mota, Miranda Brooks, *Vogue, Architectural Digest*, and Rob Haskell: thank you for your beautiful styling and for capturing Playa Grande in its glory.

Lastly, only because this is hard for me to express . . . Alexandra Jeronimo, the Playa Grande Beach Club beats with your heart. The story of the lives you have changed isn't in this book but it is the real beauty of what exists there. What we built has soul because of the abundance of yours. Fausto Batista, you lovingly created a family while tending to the entirety of the Playa Grande team and property; you are proof—in all the rainbow and unicorn ways that I'm not making light of here—that the universe does conspire to bring us what we need. While that's Ali's destiny I'm talking about, I am beyond lucky to sit under the rainbow of your marriage. Thank you both for your infinite hard work, ingenious "MacGyver-ing," all that crazy road running, and the growth and evolution you encourage in all of us through example and often just kindness. Joaquín and Paloma, thank you for sharing your family (in fact, your childhood) with us, and always adding your sparkle and energy, too. When I say "us," I mean the Playa Grande team that has become a family, whom I have been most honored to work with: Ramon Alfredo Jose, Gianilda Javier, Yinet Hernández, Vanstroig Portes, Cristian Adames, Noe Adames, and perhaps all the other Adames from Rio San Juan, Ney Lantigua, Lucy Taveras, Ania Alcequiez, Javier Castro, Carmen Liriano, Paulino, Ricardo, Bachata, and all of the beach vendors. Also, Marcel Nova, Urbania Silverio, Justin Mailloux, Esteban Vargas and his team, who get me to and from Playa Grande every time. Lastly, Dominga Frias, thank you for so many years of keeping falling coconuts off my babies, chasing down bare-bummed toddlers and faster-running preteenagers with sunblock, and forgiving them for tormenting you with snakes. I love you all.

Photography Credits

All photographs by Karyn Millet except the following:

Pages 4, 182 (top left and right), and 217 (top right) by Christopher Berdine

Pages 17 (right), 52, 153, 166, 229, and 235 by Patrick Cline

Pages 25, 50, 98, 107 (bottom right), 117, 167 (right), 182–183 (bottom), 191, 216 (top right), 226, 236–237, 248–249 (bottom center left and right) by Pip Cowley

Pages 30–31, 42–43, 45, 60–61, 86–87, 96–97, 111, 129, 149 (right), 175, 245 by Douglas Friedman

Pages 44, 53, 105, 107 (top center and right), 148, 155, 170, 183 (top left), 192, 193, 210–211 (center), 216–217 (bottom center), 222 (left), 248 (top center), 254 by Celerie Kemble

Pages 90–91, 95, 106 (bottom), 115, 199 by Francois Halard

Pages 106 (top left), 107 (top left), 131 (right), 185, 216 (bottom left) by Meghan Mehan

Pages 211 (right), 216 (top left) by Madeleine Kemble

Text Credits

Page 32: "The Old Age of Nostalgia" from ALMOST INVISIBLE: POEMS by Mark Strand, copyright © 2012 by Mark Strand. Used by permission of Alfred A. Knopf, an imprint of the Knopf Doubleday Publishing Group, a division of Penguin Random House LLC. All rights reserved.

"The Old Age of Nostalgia," currently collected in COLLECTED POEMS by Mark Strand. Copyright © 2014 by Mark Strand, used in the UK and Commonwealth by permission of The Wylie Agency LLC.

Page 90: "Forty Little Pollywogs," anonymous, available in the public domain.

Page 94: Pablo Neruda, "Oda a la luz encantada," TERCER LIBRO DE LAS ODAS © 1957, Pablo Neruda and Fundación Pablo Neruda.

"Ode to Enchanted Light" by Pablo Neruda, English translation by Mark Strand. English translation copyright © Mark Strand, used by permission of The Wylie Agency LLC.

Page 105: "The Kitchen Song" by Kimberly Cutter, all rights reserved.

Page 109: from "The Walrus and the Carpenter" by Lewis Carroll, available in the public domain.

Page 114: from "The Idea of Order at Key West," copyright © 1936 by Wallace Stevens, copyright renewed 1964 by Holly Stevens; from THE COLLECTED POEMS OF WALLACE STEVENS by Wallace Stevens. Used by permission of Alfred A. Knopf, an imprint of the Knopf Doubleday Publishing Group, a division of Penguin Random House LLC. All rights reserved. Used in the UK and Commonwealth by permission of Faber and Faber Ltd.

Page 124: Lyrics from "Playa Grande" by SOFI TUKKER & Bomba Estéreo. Written by Sophie Hawley-Weld, Tucker Halpern. Published by Third Side Music o/b/o Ticolini Music and Tukker Publishing.

"Playa Grande" written by Jon Hume [ASCAP]
Published by New Tribe Management, LLC

"Playa Grande" written by Liliana Margarita Saumet Avila
Published by EMI Blackwood Music (BMI)

"Playa Grande" written by Jose Henrique Castillo Silvera
Published by Sony/ATV Latin Music Publishing LLC (BMI)

Page 162: "Tropic Winter" by Evelyn Scott, available in the public domain.

Page 192: "The Coming of Light" from SELECTED POEMS by Mark Strand, copyright © 1979, 1980 by Mark Strand. Used by permission of Alfred A. Knopf, an imprint of the Knopf Doubleday Publishing Group, a division of Penguin Random House LLC. All rights reserved.

"The Coming of Light," currently collected in COLLECTED POEMS by Mark Strand. Copyright © 2014 by Mark Strand, used in the UK and Commonwealth by permission of The Wylie Agency LLC.

Page 214: from BEAUTY: THE INVISIBLE EMBRACE by John O'Donohue. Copyright © 2004 John O'Donohue. Used by permission of HarperCollins Publishers.

From BEAUTY: THE INVISIBLE EMBRACE by John O'Donohue. Copyright © 2004 by John O'Donohue. Used in the UK and Commonwealth by permission of Penguin Random House UK.

First published in the United States of America in 2021 by
Rizzoli International Publications, Inc.
300 Park Avenue South
New York, NY 10010
www.rizzoliusa.com

Copyright © 2021 Celerie Kemble

Photography credits and additional text credits
appear on page 255.

Publisher: Charles Miers
Editor: Aliza Fogelson
Design: Michelle Cohen /Hyphenate Design
Production Manager: Colin Hough Trapp
Managing Editor: Lynn Scrabis

Printed in Singapore

2024 2025 2026 / 10 9 8 7 6 5 4

ISBN: 978-0-8478-6219-1
Library of Congress Control Number: 2020948460

Visit us online:
Facebook.com/RizzoliNewYork
Twitter: @Rizzoli_Books
Instagram.com/RizzoliBooks
Pinterest.com/RizzoliBooks
Youtube.com/user/RizzoliNY
Issuu.com/Rizzoli